KEEP SMILING
BIRTHDAYS HAPPEN!
COLLECTORS EDITION

CELEBRITY BIRTHDAY COLOR EDITION

KEN 'DR. SMILEY' ROCHON, JR., PhD

Keep Smiling: Birthdays Happen!

© 2021 by Ken 'Dr. Smiley' Rochon, Jr., PhD

All rights reserved. No part of this publication may be reproduced or transmitted in any form or by any means, electronic or mechanical, including photocopying, recording, or by any information storage and retrieval system, without the prior written permission from the publisher or the authors, except by reviewers who may quote brief excerpts in connection with a review in a newspaper, magazine or electronic publication. Contact the publisher for information on foreign rights.

Influencer Birthday
Color Edition

ISBN: 978-1-64810-100-7

Printed in the United States of America

ACKNOWLEDGEMENTS & DEDICATIONS

The biggest joy I receive in the world is seeing my son Kenny (K3) smile. I have seen the power of his smile, and this book is my way of honoring him as well as a gentleman named Barry Shore for introducing me to the concept of 'Keep Smiling'.

Shift happens when you count your blessings, such as the people in your life who believe in you. My Dad and my wife Nelly ... Thank you!

No matter what happens in the world, you have the power to shift and when you do, you become more powerful.

Thank you to Al Granger, my brother from another mother. To Carolyn Sheltraw, my graphic designer, and to Andrea Adams-Miller, the Executive Director for the Keep Smiling Movement, and my publicist for your help with one of the most important books in the KEEP SMILING series.

PREFACE

An influencer is one of the most important and powerful responsibilities a person can have in this day and age. We, as a society, listen to influencers to make decisions on what we buy, what we like, what we love, and for what we vote. The people in this book have proven they use their influence for good.

This book is filled with over 100 influencers who generate positivity through their lifestyle choices, their messaging, and mostly through the sheer number of smiles they inspire.

Influencers who amplify goodness should be honored so they can influence even more smiles. Therefore, we created a book that helps you learn who you may want to follow and from who you may want to learn.

In a world in need of more smiles, we are so proud to honor the influencers in this book in hopes of making the world a more positive, powerful and happy place.

Every day is a gift, and when we realize someone is born on the day we are enjoying, we may find out how much better our world is because someone was born on this day that solved a big problem in the world, inspired the world and changed the world. This book includes people I have grown to admire and live because of their actions, attitude, and smiles they bring to the world.

This book celebrates a leader a day, and if you know someone you would like to nominate for a Birthday Edition, we would love to celebrate them!

Dr. Smiley :)

INTRODUCTION

My Mom brought me up to make someone feel super special on their birthday. She used to make any member of the family enjoy 'Birthday Week' to ensure she could have a party and fit baking their favorite cake and cooking their favorite meal into the schedule for that week or weekend.

A friend of mine heard about this 'Birthday week' celebration and joked that he celebrated his birthday every day. Yes, he took it to a whole new level from 'Birthday Week' to 'Birthday Year'. I thought about it and this book evolved some ten years later.

My son writes in a monthly journal called 'Celebrating Today' which was designed to remind my son that every day is a present and knowing what can be done in a day gives us an indication of what one can do with a day and a lifetime.

The people in this book are people with beautiful hearts, smiles, and souls. I recommend you connect with them, and support their joy on their birthday, and as my friend suggests… every day.

"Dear whoever is reading this: You're young, you're beautiful and someone out there is crazy about you. So smile because life is too short to be unhappy."

JANUARY 1

John Assaraf, CEO NeuroGym

John Assaraf, 2x time NY Times best-selling author, has been featured in eight movies including "The Secret." A serial entrepreneur, he consistently seeks to excel in different ways including a focus on quantum physics.

"Smiling boosts your brain power!"

JANUARY 2

JANUARY 3

Roy Smoothe

"Smiles influence abundance."

JANUARY 4

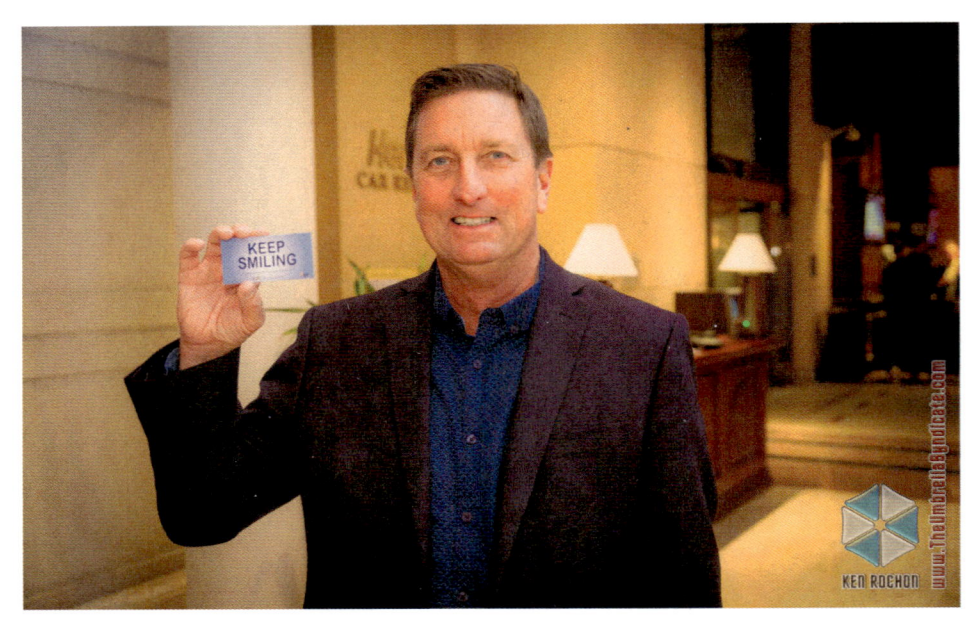

Mark Anthony Bates

"Every time you smile at someone, it is an action of love, a gift to that person, a beautiful thing."

JANUARY 5

Brian Tracy, Author

Brian Tracy is well-known businessman and motivational speaker. As an author of over seven dozen books, he leads in self-development, and he leading book is *Eat that Frog*.

"When ever you get pulled over, give the officer a *Keep Smiling* card."

JANUARY 6

JANUARY 7

Steve Farber, Author & Musician

Steve Farber is known for his leadership programs including Extreme Leadership that pushes people to excel. He released his first album after a lifelong dream of recording as a singer, songwriter, and guitar player.

"The most gorgeous feature on a woman is a knock out smile."

JANUARY 8

**Jay Abraham,
Elite Business Coach**

An international speaker, and author, Jay Abraham has impacted over 7,000 industries regarding his ability to increase corporate profitability. While know known worldwide, his initial claim to fame was direct-response marketing success in the 70's.

"Don't waste a day without smiling."

JANUARY 9

Shellie Hunt

"A smile a day keeps the opportunities in play."

JANUARY 10

Dave Farrow, Author

David Farrow is a memory celebrity having made the Canadian Guinness World Record Holder twice for Most Decks of Playing Cards Memorized in a Single Sighting. He is a speaker and memory coach.

"Music and smiles are the best mix of life."

JANUARY 11

Naomi Judd

Naomi Judd is an American country music singer and actress

"For every one smile you give, is a smile that is given to so many beyond that moment."

JANUARY 12

Diane Halfman

"A gentle word, a kind look, a good-natured smile can work wonders and accomplish miracles." –William Hazlitt

JANUARY 13

JANUARY 14

Carl Weathers

Carl Weathers, professional football player turned actor is most known as Apollo Creed in *Rocky* and George Dillon in the thriller, *Predator*.

"If you do not have a smile, I will give you one of mine."

JANUARY 15

Olivia Black

"Raise a child with smiles and it will follow them through life." ~ Ken Rochon, Jr.

JANUARY 16

Leggra Colon, Speaker

"Speak with a smile and your communication with inspire listeners."

JANUARY 17

Jane Deuber

"You smiled at the stars like they knew all your secrets."

JANUARY 18

Otis OJ Anderson-

"It's Smile Time!"

JANUARY 19

Tennille Morris

"Remember to smile." – Nelson Mandela

JANUARY 20

Buzz Aldrin, Retired Astronaut

Buzz Aldrin is an iconic hero most notably known as one the first men on the moon due to his piloting the Lunar Landing during the Apollo 11 mission.

"I hope you always find a reason to smile."

JANUARY 21

Devin Scott

"Because of your smile, you make life more beautiful." ~Thich Nhat Hanh

Dr. Will Moreland

"A smile is a metaphysical phenomenon that shifts humanity every time it is experienced."

JANUARY 23

JANUARY 24

Sean R. Callagy

"Always remember to be happy because you never know who's falling in love with your smile."

JANUARY 25

Jose Escobar

"Give 'em that razzle dazzle smile!"

JANUARY 26

Carlos Siqueira

"Smiles Influence the world and create a positive frequency."

JANUARY 27

Jay Fiset

"Smile captured is a memory for life."

JANUARY 28

Dr. Sarah Langley

"Wellness happens when we think and grow smiles."

JANUARY 29

Bob Burg, Author, Speaker

"It is always a good time to smile,
no matter what time zone you are in."

JANUARY 30

Steven Gaffney, Author, Speaker

"The transformation of a smile"

JANUARY 31

Adam Wilber

"Your smile is a choice, make it often."

FEBRUARY 1

Leo Climaco

"If you smile when no one else is around, you really mean it." – Andy Rooney

FEBRUARY 2

Lance Allred

"A smile informs the world you are a person that welcomes happiness and also delivers it."

FEBRUARY 3

Dom Faussette

"Smile with Style."

FEBRUARY 4

Lawrence Taylor

"Smiling is smart, that is just common sense."

FEBRUARY 5

Lowell Sheets

"You never get a chance to make a first impression... Just smile!"

FEBRUARY 6

John Hope Bryant

"Smiles can cause you to climb mountains."

FEBRUARY 7

Noah St John

"Smiles are the soul food of your mood."

FEBRUARY 8

Dr. James Dentley

"Leaders measure their impact in smiles."

FEBRUARY 9

Terayle Marquis Hill, Actor

"Smiles create a future of smiles."

FEBRUARY 10

Jenny Powers

"If you smile at someone, they might smile back."

FEBRUARY 11

Amy Wake

"A smile confuses an approaching frown."

FEBRUARY 12

Jesse Cruz

"Smiles make you jolly."

FEBRUARY 13

Coach Ken Carter

"Have a colorful smile to enhance your look."

FEBRUARY 14

Pat O'Brien

"Smile everyday and live longer."

FEBRUARY 15

Demond Nicholson, Boxer

"A gentleman smiles at the opportunity to make the world better."

FEBRUARY 16

Paula Fellingham

"SharSmile at Opportunity."

FEBRUARY 17

Les Brown, Author, Speaker

"Even a smile is a good deed."
–Shari Arison

FEBRUARY 18

John Travolta, Actor

John Travolta, an actor, singer, and dancer became most notable as a sex idol after his appearance in Saturday Night Fever. Years later, he reinvigorated his heart throb appeal by his portrayal of Danny in Grease, co-starring with Olivia Newton John. Additionally, he was loved as the comedic Vinny Barbarino in Welcome Back Kotter.

> "Dancing is part of the soul and makes people smile."

FEBRUARY 19

Cemo Basen

"Class clowns cause smiles."

FEBRUARY 20

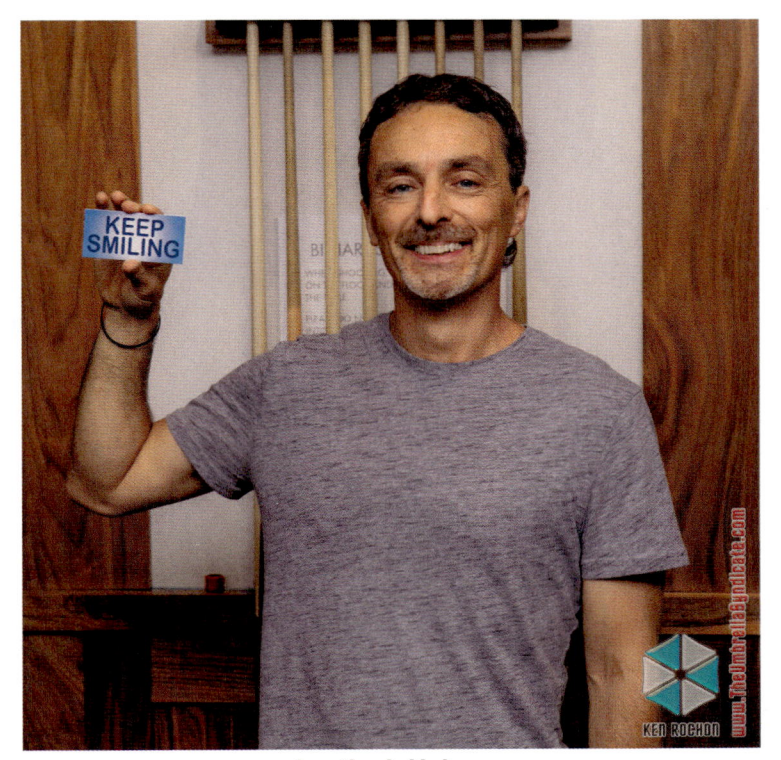

Austin J. Haines

"Most smiles are started by another smile."

FEBRUARY 21

Stormy Wellington

"Smiles are Significant!"

FEBRUARY 22

Brent Stone

"Smiling is smart, that is just common sense."

FEBRUARY 23

Daymond John, SharkTank & FUBU Founder

Daymond John is an astute businessman, most known for his role on SharkTank. He is a clothing designer, investor, author, and motivational speaker.

"Take on every challenge with a smile and you have already increased your chances of success."

Walter O'Brien

Walter O'Brien has one of the highest IQs noted, and his knack for information technology has been the inspiration for the Hit TV show *Scorpion*.

"Glorious food brings smiles to your soul."

FEBRUARY 25

Antoine Chevalier

"The Smile Hunter."

FEBRUARY 26

Anna Pereira

"Trying changing the world with a Smile."

FEBRUARY 27

Gualter Amarelo

"Amazing smiles attract amazing customers."

FEBRUARY 28

Randi Zuckerberg

"A beautiful person with a beautiful smile gives us reason to smile."

FEBRUARY 29

MARCH 1

Gretchen Downey

"Think Yourself Happy with a Smile."

MARCH 2

D. Bliss Verrengia, Speaker

A leader of women, D. Bliss Verrengia, founded Make, Save, & Invest Money Online and leads the Porsche's & Purses online community.

"A smile a day keeps the opportunities in play."

MARCH 3

Hershal Walker, Athlete

Herschel Walker is a football Hall of Fame honoree who formerly played for four NFL teams as a running back. He is now a motivational speaker. He is still in the top ten for all-purpose yardage covered.

"Smiles Influence the world and create a positive frequency."

MARCH 4

Landon Timothy Donovan, USMNT

American professional soccer player who plays for Major Arena Soccer League side San Diego Sockers. He holds numerous individual records in Major League Soccer and for the United States national team and is regarded as one of the greatest U.S. men's soccer players of all time.

"Even with all my imperfections I can still SMILE!"

MARCH 5

Nita Patel

"Making someone smile can change the world. Maybe not the whole world, but their own world."

MARCH 6

Sarah Victory

"Take a smile challenge often and see how many smiles you can create in an hour."

MARCH 7

Kenny Aronoff

"Smiles are communicated through the phone as if you were speaking face to face."

MARCH 8

Dr. Clint Rogers

"Make it your goal in life is to cause people dance, sing and smile and you will be a hero to many!"

MARCH 9

Erin Ley

"Smiles cause trust funnels of abundance."

MARCH 10

JJ Villar

"When a smile is given to you, be grateful and return it as often as possible."

MARCH 11

Kameren Dawson

"Keep smiling because life is a beautiful thing, and there is so much to smile about"
~Marilyn Monroe

MARCH 12

AJ Smith

"Never regret anything that made you smile."

MARCH 13

Karen Owens

"The One Smile you give, can be the smile that makes all the difference."

Quincy Jones, Legendary Record Producer

Quincy Jones, jazz musician, a revered icon as a music producer and composer received 79 Grammy nominations and winner of 27.

"Everywhere you go, take a smile with you."

MARCH 15

Bret Michaels, Musician

Brett Michaels is the songwriter and lead singer for Poison, the rock band. Their top song was *Every Rose Has Its Thorn* as well as *Talk Dirty to Me*.

"The American Dream is built one smile at a time."

MARCH 16

Amberly Brown Lago

"Smile and it will jazz up your life."

MARCH 17

Aidan Uttinger

"Never lose your inner smile."

MARCH 18

Becca Tebon

"Your smile will impact and open doors to higher vibration. Share it freely with others ... And with yourself every day! " ~ Becca Tebon

MARCH 19

Misty Bright

"Strong people know how to keep their life in order. Even with tears in their eyes, they still manage to say "I'm okay" with a smile."

MARCH 20

Manny Lopez, Founder of ServeX

"Victory comes to those who smile."

MARCH 21

Grant Cardone

Grant Cardone amassed a large following due to his success as an Internet Marketer. He is the author of the bestselling books *The 10X Rule* and *If You're Not First, You're Last.*

"Smile and the world smiles with you."
–Stanley Gordon West

MARCH 22

Linda Bruns

"To create a better future, smile in the present."
– Ken Rochon, Jr.

MARCH 23

Shirley Luu

"You are somebody's reason to smile."

MARCH 24

Mali Phonpadith

"Smiles launch leaders to success."
~ Ken Rochon, Jr.

MARCH 25

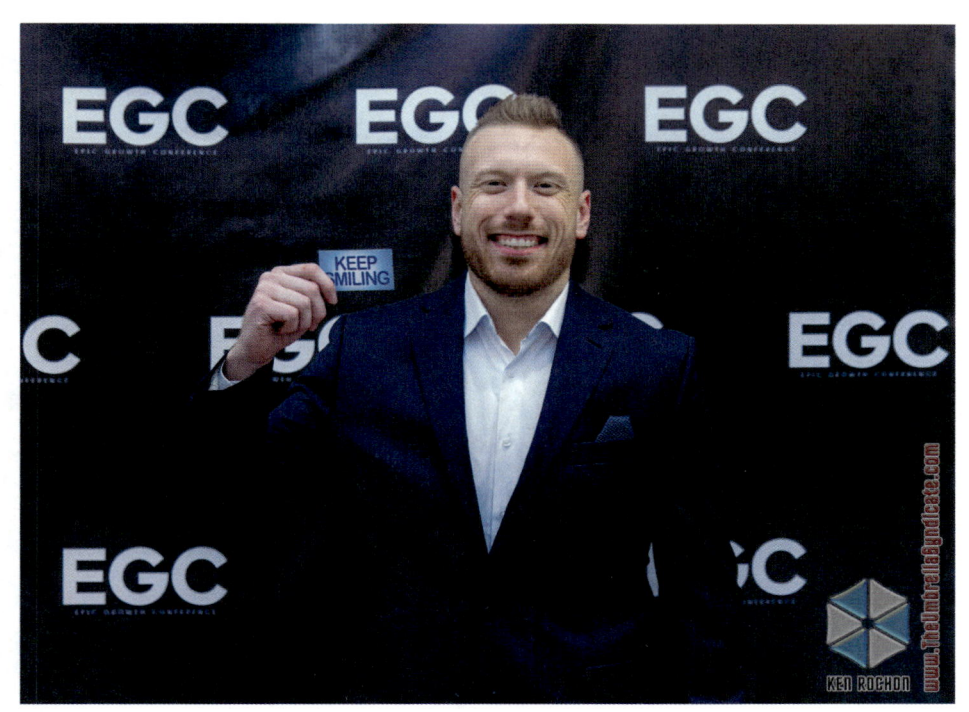

Tyler Cerny

"But God can only smile because only God can show what is coming next." ~ Desmund Tutu

MARCH 26

Leeza Gibbons

"Have a Turbo Charged Smile."

MARCH 27

MARCH 28

Ouiwey Collins, Singer

"Be the reason someone smiles today."

MARCH 29

Elle MacPherson

Elle Macpherson, model, is most known for her bikini-clad covers for the *Sports Illustrated* Swimsuit Issues. Additional, she has appeared in multiple movies and is an astute businesswoman, too.

"Feel free to smile and connect."

MARCH 30

MARCH 31

Helice 'Grandma Sparky' Bridges, You Make a Difference

"Smile, it is the key that fits the lock to everybody's heart." ~ Anthony J. D' Angelo

APRIL 1

Michael Maloney

"A smile costs less than electricity, but gives more light. So always smile, and prove that you are the best bulb in the world."

APRIL 2

Jerry DJSkeeper Cleo

"Cause the pendulum of a frown into a smile."

APRIL 3

Ryan Mauldin, Speaker

"A beautiful smile is your best asset."

APRIL 4

APRIL 5

APRIL 6

Mandy White Eskelin

"Keep smiling no matter what is going on in your life."

APRIL 7

James Lawrence, World Record Triathlete

James Lawrence ran over 30 triathlons including Iron length distances in a single year which make him a world record triathlete.

"You Will Change The World with a Smile."

APRIL 8

APRIL 9

APRIL 10

APRIL 11

Tai Lopez, Entrepreneur

Tai Lopez, serial entrepreneur, has always been a risk taker. He now advises 20+ multi-millionaire businesses. Tai is an avid speaker and podcaster who inspires others to achieve their highest capability in all aspects of their lives.

"The strength of a smile shows character and confidence. Don't let any one bully you out of your smile."

APRIL 12

APRIL 13

John Paul DeJoria

John Paul Jones DeJoria became a billionaire based on his entrepreneurship and his co-founded company "Paul Mitchell" as well as "Patron Spirits."

"Smile despite the circumstances and laugh throughout the pain. Life is full of hardships but it is how you deal with them that will define you."

Tracy Repchuk

"Stay strong. Make them wonder how you're still smiling."

APRIL 15

Maria Matarelli

"A smile captured in a photo will spread happiness forever."

APRIL 16

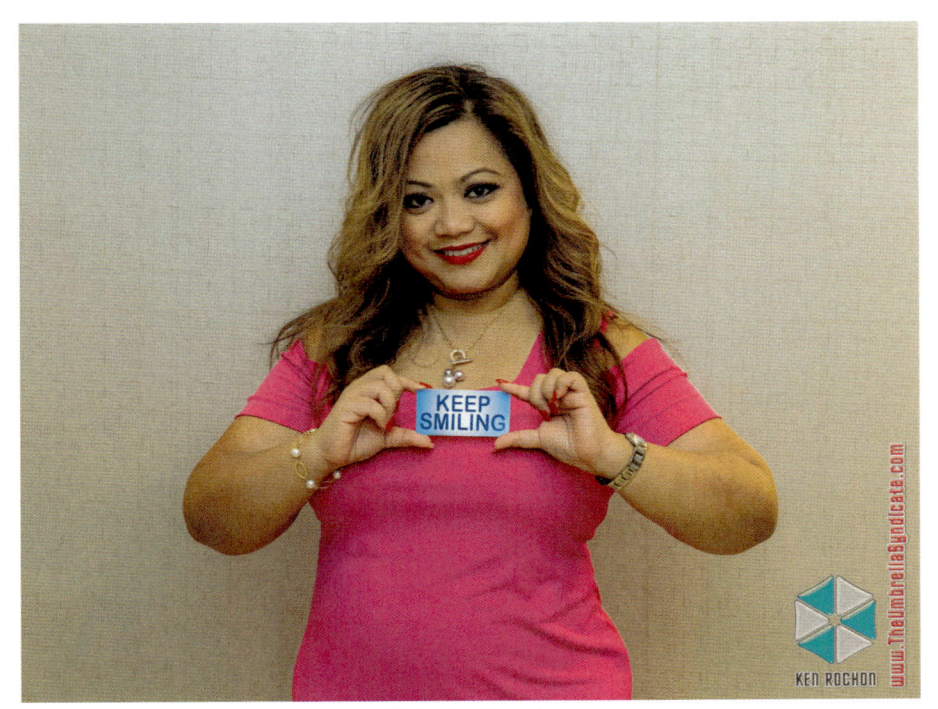

Melody Garcia

"The pot of gold isn't necessarily at the end of the rainbow. It's at the beginning of your smile."

APRIL 17

APRIL 18

APRIL 19

Mark Volman, The Turtles

"Smile with kindness and watch the abundance it influences."

APRIL 20

George Takei, Actor

George Hosato Takei, actor, is most known for his portrayal of Hikaru Sulu, helmsman of the USS Enterprise in the long running television series *Star Trek*.

"Making someone smile can change the world. Maybe not the whole world, but their own world."

APRIL 21

Joy Cooper Willett

"Cover your mouth when you cough, not when you smile."

APRIL 22

Huey Scott

"It takes seventeen muscles to smile and forty-three to frown."

APRIL 23

David Tutera, Wedding Planner, Speaker

David Tutera is one of the most famous celebrity wedding planners in the world. As a professional speaker and bridal fashion designer, he hosts several television programs and has penned multiple books on the subject.

"Every smile makes you a day younger."

APRIL 24

Neil Patel, Marketer

Neil Patel is the co-founder of *Crazy Egg, Hello Bar* and *KISSmetrics*. He consults with Fortune 500 companies like *Amazon, NBC, GM, HP,* and *Viacom* grow their revenue. He is noted as one of the top influencer's on the web by the *Wall Street Journal* and as Forbes one of top 10 Online Marketers.

> "Well, it's on'n'on'n'on on'n'on,
> I smile to the break of dawn."

APRIL 25

Clarissa Burt, Author

This powerhouse acts, models, emcees, speaks, writes, produces and more. She has graced over 100 magazine covers and is known for The Never Ending Story.

"The greatest gift is a smile at the right time."

APRIL 26

CSM Donnell Johns, Veterans Growing America

"Try smiling while your heart aches, even laughing through the pain, for tomorrow is a brand new day and the sun will rise again."

APRIL 27

Dr. Robert Cialdini, Founder & CEO, Influence at Work

Robert Cialdini, a prolific business copywriter and fantastic marketer, he has amassed millions of followers for his advice in marketing and publicity due to the book *Influence: The Psychology of Persuasion*.

"A SMILE only requires one muscle... exercise it."

Robert Clancy, Author & Speaker

As a speaker and best-selling author of *The Hitch-hiker's Guide to the Soul*, Robert Clancy has led millions to seek spiritual awakening.

"Beer, Cheers, Smile"

APRIL 29

APRIL 30

MAY 1

George C. Fraser

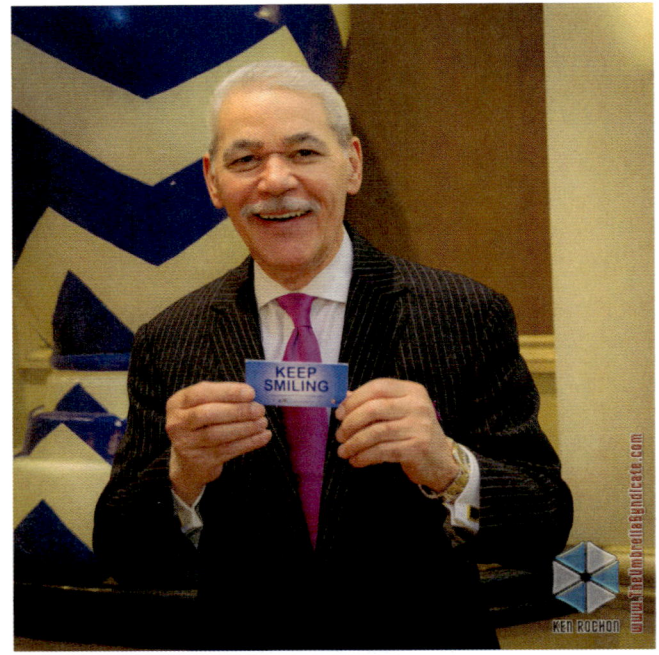

George C. Fraser led a Global Networking Movement to generate a "Success-Guide Worldwide: The Networking Guide to Black Resources" in which he changes the lives of African Americans.

"Smile like you want to make millions."

MAY 2

Dr. Sher Mathew

"Smile to the Moon and Beyond!"

MAY 3

Terha Watterson

"Smile is electricity and life is battery. Whenever you smile, the battery gets charged and a beautiful life is activated. So keep smiling."

MAY 4

Andrea Adams Miller

"Smile at adversity and that will throw a curve ball at how you approach any challenge."

MAY 5

Joel Comm

"Smile a little more. Regret a little less."

MAY 6

Maimah Karmo

"Smile everyday and live longer."

MAY 7

MAY 8

Dame Lillian Walker

"The world always looks brighter from behind a smile."

MAY 9

Harry Lay, CEO

"Focus on giving smiles away and you will discover that your own smiles will always be in great supply."

MAY 10

Ilana Bissonnette

"Smile and you are a Super Star!"

MAY 11

MAY 12

Steve Smilth Sr.

"The Impact of a Smile is Powerful."

MAY 13

MAY 14

Dr. Cheryl Lentz

"Make a Wish... Make a Smile."

MAY 15

Ray Lewis, Baltimore Ravens NFL Football Linebacker

Ray Lewis, NFL Linebacker, received the distinction of MVP in 2000 who has been part of two (2) Superbowl wins. He is in the Football Hall of Fame.

"Even if you get sidelined, don't let your smile be injured as it will get you back on the field quickest."

MAY 16

MAY 17

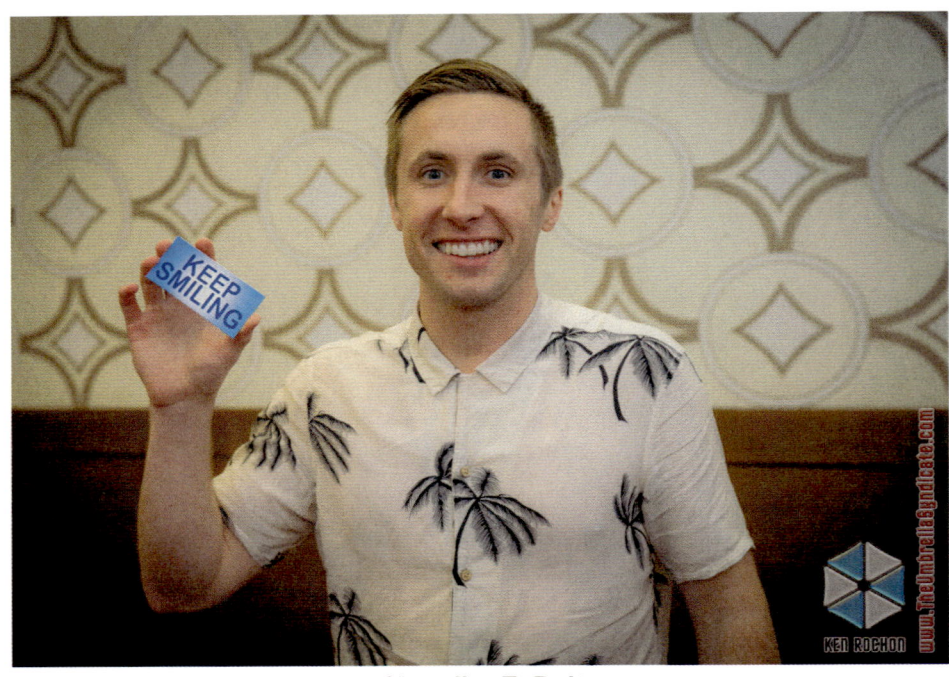

Chandler E. Bolt

"A smile shows the reflection of your mindset and spirit."

MAY 18

Maggy Fancy Francois

"The best thing to schedule on your calendar is a smile and everything else will fall into place"
— Ken Rochon, Jr.

MAY 19

Sid Peddinti

"When you smile, the whole world stops and stares for a while."

MAY 20

Robert Allen

"Leaders measure their impact in smiles."

MAY 21

MAY 22

Dr. Vinny Leonti

"Your body makes you sexy. Your smile makes you pretty. But your personality makes you beautiful."

MAY 23

Thorald Koren

"Shift Lanes and Smile more!"

MAY 24

Summer Dey

"A warm smile is the universal language of kindness." –William Arthur Ward

MAY 25

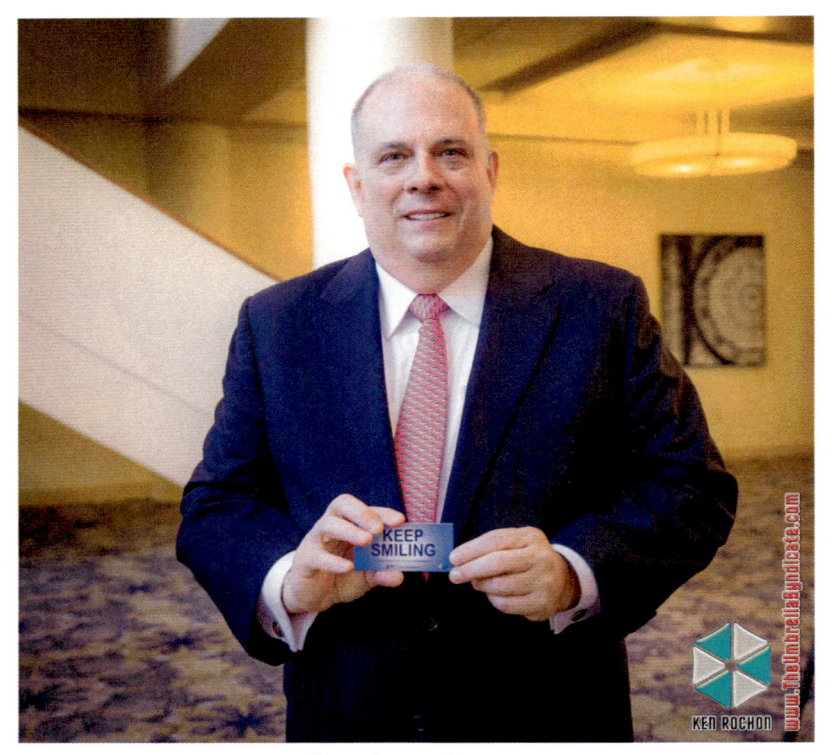

Gov. Larry Hogan

"Mission: Smile America!"

MAY 26

Pam Grier, Foxy Brown

"The Secret to Happiness is to Keep Smiling."

MAY 27

Jim Koch, Founder of Samuel Adams, Author & Speaker

Jim Koch, Harvard graduate with a BA, MBA, & a JD, co-founded the Boston Beer Company, the producers of Samuel Adams beer. While schooled through high academia, he says he gained more about creating a successful business from books by Tom Hopkins than all his professional degrees.

"The best smile is the best value to your face."

MAY 28

Jackson Strong

"Be a Beast and Smile!"

MAY 29

MAY 30

Kenny Harper, Author & Speaker

"Smile, it's better than a poke in the eye."
– Douglas Horton

MAY 31

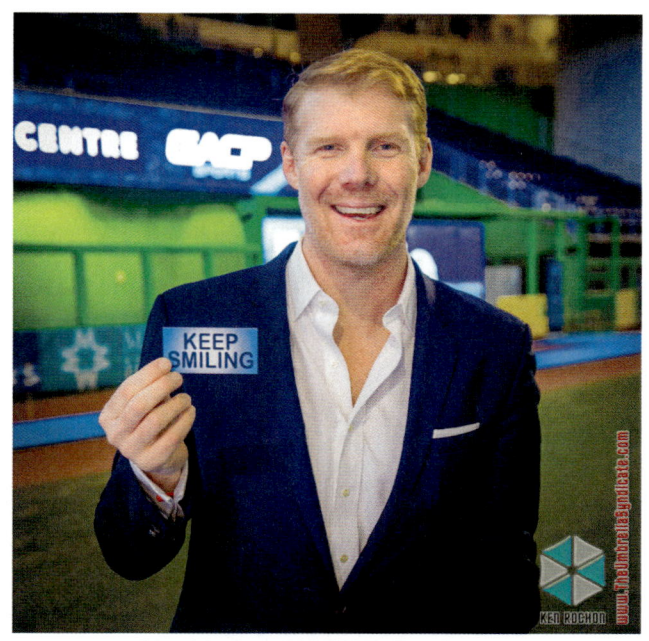

Alexi Lalas, USMNT, FoxSports

American retired soccer player who played mostly as a defender. Lalas is best known for his participation with the United States men's national soccer team in the 1994 FIFA World Cup, where he was a standout player on the team with his distinctive long beard and hair.

"Smile and you will wow them all the time."

JUNE 2

Gerald Patrick Mathers, Actor ' Leave It to Beaver'

"When people are smiling they are most receptive to almost anything you want to teach them." – Allen Funt

JUNE 3

Paula 'Pixie' Dezzutti

"Keep smiling, you're beautiful."

JUNE 4

Dr. Steve Taubman

"Smiling doesn't always mean you're happy with everything. Sometimes it just means you're strong enough to accept it and make the best of it.

JUNE 5

Gina Gaudio-Graves

"Your body, mind and soul are more balanced when you include a smile in your expression."
~ Ken Rochon, Jr.

JUNE 6

JUNE 7

Mark Porteous

"Q. How do you get a mouse to smile?
A. Say cheese!!"

JUNE 8

Chuck Negron, Three Dog Night

"The more you smile, the more mojo you exude."

JUNE 9

JUNE 10

Laura Clark

"Smiles create a bug free mind capable of masterminding with the best."

JUNE 11

Dr. Brett Lane aka 'Dr. Digital'

"A smile can brighten the darkest day."

JUNE 12

Robert Angel

"Smiles cause trust funnels of abundance."

JUNE 13

Titus Showers

"When life gives you limes,
rearrange the letters until they say smile."

JUNE 14

Anik Singal

"Raise a child with smiles and it will follow them through life."

JUNE 15

Guy "Master Gee" O'Brien

"Beauty is power; a smile is its sword."
~ John Ray

JUNE 16

Ben Ward, Author

"Do something special for someone today: just give them a smile and you will be amazed at how much of a difference it makes."

JUNE 17

Joe Piscopo, Actor, Author & Comedian

Joe Piscopo, actor and comedian, is most noted for his comedic talent on *Saturday Night Live*. He impersonates more than 50 personalities.

"Smile and you live, smile and you attract love, laugh uncontrollably when you smile and you are crazy."

JUNE 18

Dupé Aleru

"A smile is one of the best forms of flattery."

JUNE 19

Ken Davitian, Actor

As a comedic actor, Ken Davitian is most notable for his role as Borat's producer in the film *Borat*.

"Unfrowns are Smiles that have not been inverted."

Michael Gerber, Author

Michael Gerber, best-selling author, *The E-Myth*, has been honored by *Inc. Magazine* as *The World's #1 Small Business Guru*.

"Smiling will charge up your day because it is electrifying!"

Rudy Mawer

"Look back, and smile on perils past."
–Walter Scott

JUNE 22

Jehanne de Champvallon

"A smile is a universal welcome."

JUNE 23

Brandon Steiner

"Every time you smile at someone, it is an action of love, a gift to that person, a beautiful thing."

JUNE 24

Shep Hyken, Author

"Start every day with a smile and get it over with." ~ W.C. Fields

JUNE 25

Lyman A. Montgomery, Author & Speaker

"Smile and you will wow them all the time."

JUNE 26

Harper Grace

"Smile and Don't Quit!"

JUNE 27

Doni Glover

"Let your smile change the world,
but don't let the world change your smile."

JUNE 28

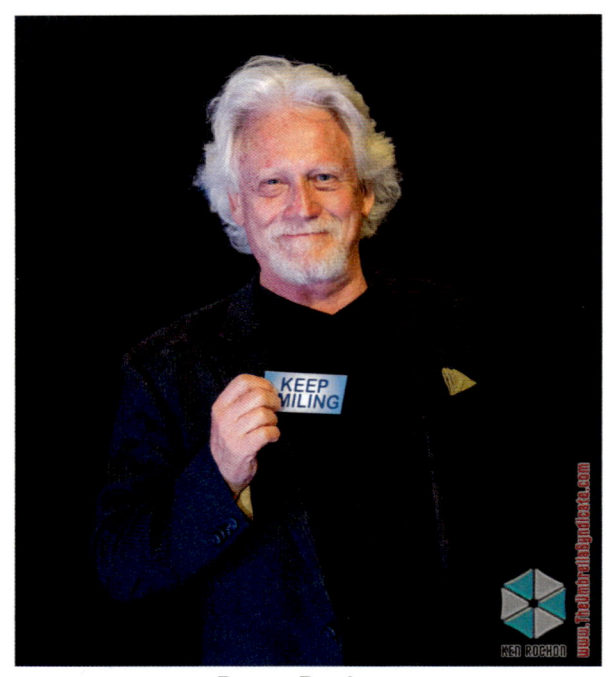

Bruce Davison

An American actor and director of television, film, and theater. Davison is well known for his starring role as Willard Stiles in the cult horror films Willard.

"Leaders Smile!"

JUNE 29

William Gary Busey, Actor

"The fact that I can plant a seed and it becomes a flower, share a bit of knowledge and it becomes another's, smile." – Leo Buscaglia

JUNE 30

Dr. Ivan Misner, Founder of BNI, Author, Speaker

"Smile so big and so much that it makes people say 'Wow!'"

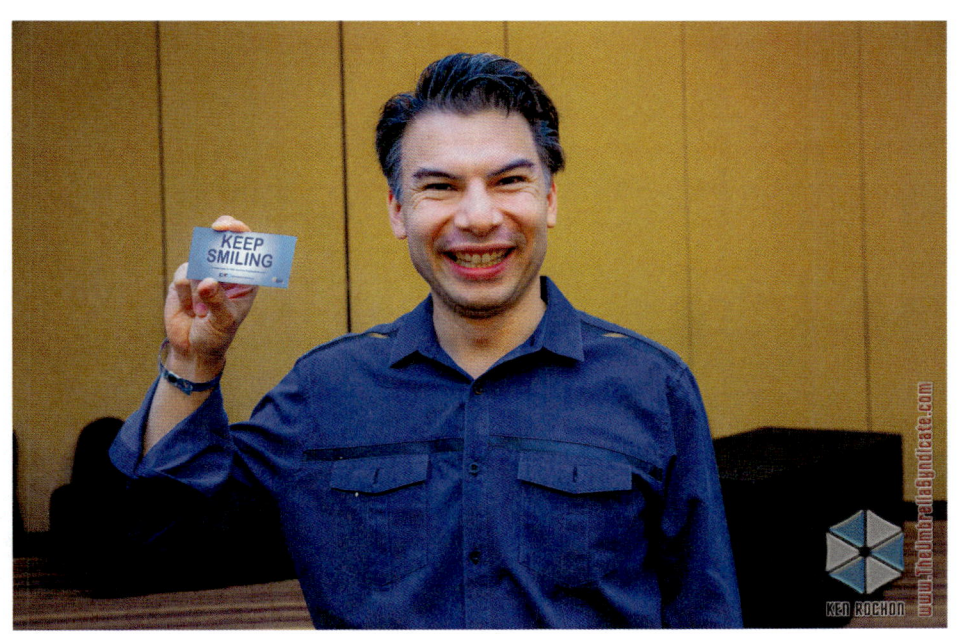

Jon Block

"It's amazing how people still can smile that show smile when they are pushing it to extremes due to the rush of adrenaline."

JULY 2

Tony Horton, Founder P90x

Tony Horton, personal trainer, is best known for his infomercials showcasing P90x, a home fitness program that pushes physical extremes.

"If you are too busy to smile, you are too busy."

JULY 3

Dan Henry

"Keep smiling… and one day life will get tired of upsetting you."

JULY 4

Andrew Zimmern, Food Celebrity

Andrew Scott Zimmern has dabbled his palate in just about everything related to media, travel and food most interestingly known for the *Bizarre World of Food* and *Go Fork Yourself* where food pushes the limit.

"A smile is your authentic brand."

JULY 5

Claudia Wells

"Nothing is more beautiful than a smile that has struggled through tears." ~Demi Lovato

JULY 6

Rey 👑 Perez

"Smiling is the Best Idea!"

JULY 8

Toby Keith

American country singer, songwriter, actor, and record producer. Keith released his first four studio albums—1993's Toby Keith, 1994's Boomtown, 1996's Blue Moon and 1997's Dream Walkin', plus a Greatest Hits package for various divisions of Mercury.

"A smile a day keeps the opportunities in play."

JULY 9

Dr. Craig Coates

"Smile to Infinity and beyond!"

Robert Pine

An American actor who is best known as Sgt. Joseph Getraer on the television series *CHiPs*.

"No matter where you go in the world, you will find a smile is the universal expression."

JULY 11

JULY 12

Corinne Hancock, Speaker

"A need a smile like I need air."

JULY 13

José Andrés, President / Chef Think Food Group

José Andrés, noted as one of Time Magazine's top 100 Influential people, is a world-renowned Chef. This culinary artist teaches at George Washington as well as Harvard. An advocate for ending hunger, he started World Central Kitchen to feed the hungry and empower those in crisis.

"A Smile is the best way to hypnotize the world to respond with happiness."

JULY 14

JULY 15

Stephen Howard

"'S' is for Smile!"

JULY 16

Werner Berger, Guinness World Record Holder, Author & Speaker

"Children learn to smile from their parents."
– Shinichi Suzuki

JULY 17

Ken McArthur, Speaker

"When music touches the heart, a smile soon follows."

JULY 18

Angel Tuccy

"Beautiful Smile... Beautiful Life"

JULY 19

JULY 20

Jay Jay French

"Swing that frown pendulum to a Smile."

JULY 21

Michael Bernard Beckwith, New Thought Minister

Michael Bernard Beckwith, founder of the Agape International Spiritual Center, is an author, minister, and spiritual advisor. He was featured in several spiritual films including *The Secret*.

"I am an Advocate of Smiling."

JULY 22

Gift Hughes

"Leadership is best shown with a confident smile."

Daniel Pink, Author & Speaker

Daniel Pink, former speech writer for Al Gore, combines research on social behavior and workplace engineering to devise methods to increase efficiency and reduce discourse. He wrote the best-selling book *To Sell Is Human, Drive, and A Whole New Mind.*

"Smiling makes a fashion statement."

JULY 24

Dr. Nate Salah

"When we smile, we conquer doubt, fear, sadness and worry."

JULY 25

MJ McFarland

"Smile everyday and live longer."

JULY 26

Leah Roling, Speaker

"Peace begins with a smile."

JULY 27

JULY 28

Scott Parazynsky

"A Smile Brightens Your face."

210

JULY 29

JULY 30

Jewels Muller

"If you have teeth, then Keep Smiling... or I will bash them in and give you something to smile about."

JULY 31

David Bayer

"A smile is the prettiest thing you'll ever wear."

AUGUST 1

Artis Leon Ivey Jr., AKA Coolio

"Unfrowns are Smiles that have not been inverted."

AUGUST 2

Butch Patrick

"A smile is the lighting system of the face, the cooling system of the head, and the heating system of the heart."

AUGUST 3

Isaiah Washington

"The invention of the Keep Smiling card gave everyone something to hold and smile about."

AUGUST 4

Dr. Greg S. Reid, Author, Speaker

"A smile is the shortest distance between two people."

AUGUST 5

Ken 'Dr. Smiley' Rochon, Jr.

"A smile amplifies goodness." – Ken Rochon

AUGUST 6

David Wolfe, Health Advocate

David "Avocado" Wolfe is one of the most followed health advocates followed by a number of celebrities. Currently, he is a beekeeper, chocolate farmer, vanilla grower, and Nutribullet spokesperson advocating for raw food.

> "Smiles are the universal expression of positive connection."

AUGUST 7

AUGUST 8

Larry Wilcox

An American actor best known for his role as California Highway Patrol officer Jonathan "Jon" Baker in television series CHiPs, which ran from 1977 to 1983 in which he was assigned "7 Mary 3" and became partners with Francis Llewelyn "Ponch" Poncherello.

"Keep smiling and be fearless!"

AUGUST 9

Peter Michael Blicharz

"If you do not start out the day with a smile, it is not too late to start practicing for tomorrow."

AUGUST 10

Angel Ribo

"Smiles speak volumes."

AUGUST 11

AUGUST 12

Kyle Arrington

"To smile is human."

AUGUST 13

Dr. Freeman Hrabowski III, President of UMBC

"Let your smile change the world, but don't let the world change your smile."

# AUGUST 14

Ashkan Tabibnia

"Smile, it lets your teeth breathe."

AUGUST 15

Carl Gould

"Sometimes life has a tendency to wipe away a smile; God has a tendency to keep you smiling."

AUGUST 16

Rev. Dr. George E. Holmes

"A kind heart is a fountain of gladness, making everything in its vicinity freshen into smiles."
—Washington Irving

Amberlyn White

"Smile, it's free therapy."

AUGUST 18

Lizzie Ens, Author & Speaker

"I am an Advocate of Smiling."

Jack Canfield, Author

Thought leader, keynote speaker, and business success coach, Jack Canfield fosters excellence through *The Success Principles*.

"Feel free to smile and connect."

AUGUST 20

AUGUST 21

Rudy Ruettiger

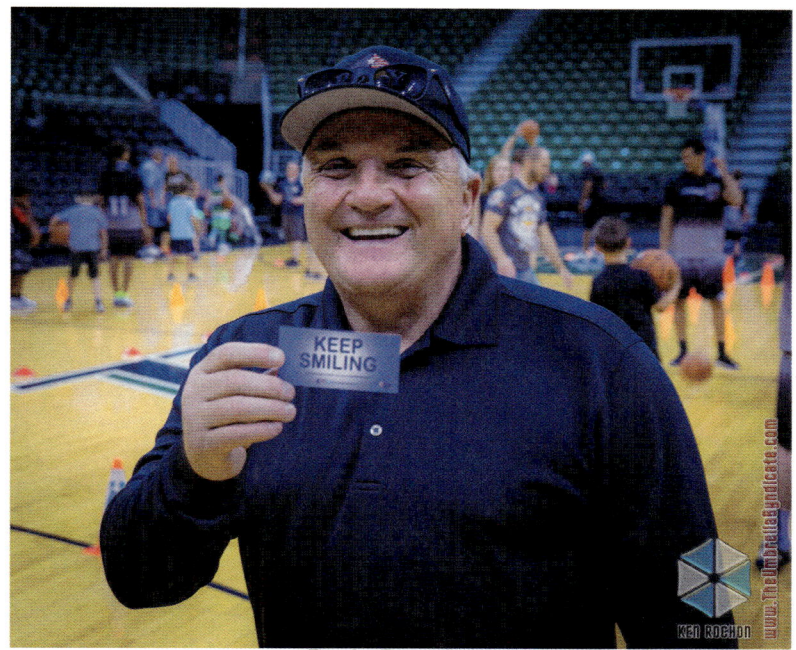

"Rudy" Ruettiger, a motivational speaker, wrote the script for the hit film "Rudy" based on his experience playing college football at the University of Notre Dame.

"A smile is never misunderstood as anything but happiness and love."

AUGUST 23

AUGUST 24

Aaron Velky

"Smiles make you feel like a Knight in Shining Armor"

237

AUGUST 25

Roxie Griego

"But God can only smile because only God can know what is coming next." – Desmond Tutu

AUGUST 26

AUGUST 27

Teri Miller

"Why did the Chicken cross the road with his Soup? To Smile on the Other Side."

AUGUST 28

Luis Guzmán, Actor

"Rockin' & Smilin'."

AUGUST 29

Ajit Nawalkha

"Sometimes the best revenge is just a simple smile, to let them know you're doing just fine."

AUGUST 30

Frank Kern, Internet Marketer

Frank Kern, Direct Response Internet Marketing consultant, he focuses on utilizing excellent skills in copywriting combined with automated behavioral response which converts websites to profit effectively.

When you are not feeling powerful, shift and accept your love and power to smile."

AUGUST 31

Brian Kelly

"Smile with confidence and attract abundance."

SEPTEMBER 1

Dan Fleyshman

"Keep smiling and brighten someone's day."

SEPTEMBER 2

Daniela Peeler, Mrs. Maryland

"Every smile has a silver lining"

SEPTEMBER 3

Ron LeGrand

"Don't forget to smile."

SEPTEMBER 4

Dr. Lotus Riché

"Always wear a smile, because your smile is a reason for many others to smile."

SEPTEMBER 5

Dr. Rich Castellano

"You're braver than you believe, stronger than you seem, and smarter than you think... and inspire more smiles than you know."

SEPTEMBER 6

Jay Ghanashyam Shetty

"When a smile is given to you, be grateful and return it as often as possible."

SEPTEMBER 7

Andre Berto, Boxing Champion

"When I saw you, I fell in love, and you smiled because you knew" – William Shakespeare

SEPTEMBER 8

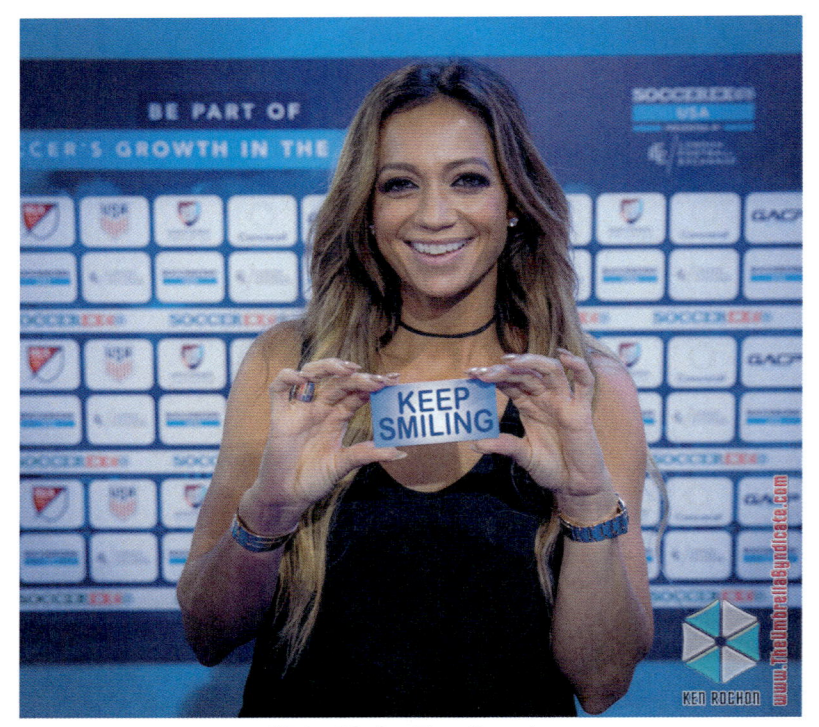

Kate Abdo, Fox Sports

"The Ubiquitous Smile will connect you to people creating magic in the world."

252

SEPTEMBER 9

Gizelle Bryant, The Real Housewives of Potomac – Bravo TV

Gizelle Bryant is the CEO of *EveryHue Beauty* cosmetics and a philanthropist most known for her appearance on *The Real Housewives of Potomac*.

"A smile unites the world much like a song with a contagious beat causes the world to dance."

SEPTEMBER 10

Ron Blackburn

"A Smile is the best way to hypnotize the world to respond with happiness."

SEPTEMBER 11

Jeff Parker, Co-Founder of Aurea

"A smile is happiness you'll find right under your nose." —Tom Wilson

SEPTEMBER 12

Dr. Kara Scott Dentley, Speaker

"The absolute best gift you can give someone is a smile, it is like music to the soul."

SEPTEMBER 13

Marieo Foster

"The absolute best gift you can give someone is a smile, it is like music to the soul."

SEPTEMBER 14

Bill Walsh

"A smile can hide so many feelings, fear, sadness, heartbreak, but it also shows one other thing, strength."

SEPTEMBER 15

Lt. General Russel L. Honoré, Author & Speaker

Retired Military Leader, Lt. General Russel Honoré, commanded the joint task force for Category 5 Hurricane Katrina making controversial decisions that saved people and gave America hope.

"We shall never know all the good that a simple smile can do. " – Mother Teresa

Dr. Bill Dorfman, Celebrity Dentist & Best-Selling Author

Dr. Bill Dorfman, author of *Billion Dollar Smile,* founded *Zoom* whitening, the most utilized dental product around. A philanthropist, he oversees The Leap Foundation which leads kids to adopt professional skills that exemplify greatness. He is a frequent guest of T*he Doctors*

"Add Smile to your diet and live vivaciously."

SEPTEMBER 17

Clifton Crosby

"A picture is worth a thousand words but a SMILE from someone you love is worth a thousand Rembrandt's ...." ~Gary C. Clark

SEPTEMBER 18

SEPTEMBER 19

Austin LeFevre

"A bank of smiles leads to more abundance in the bank."

SEPTEMBER 20

Sara Bee, Model

"Smiling is contagious!"

SEPTEMBER 21

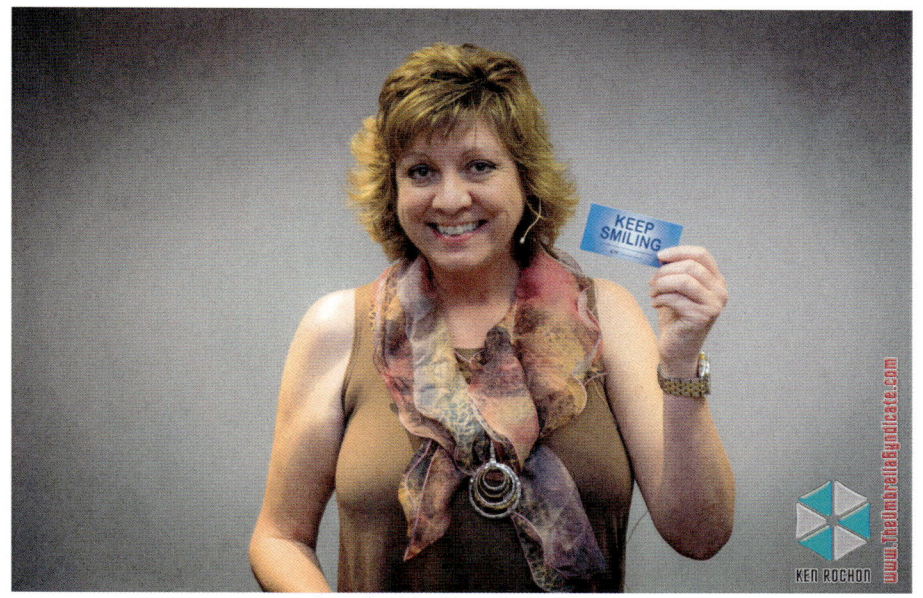

Stephanie Frank, Author

As a trained behavioral profiler and cyber intelligence officer, Stephanie Frank shows business clients how to accomplish personal and professional success.

"Let your smile change the world,
but don't let the world change your smile."

SEPTEMBER 22

Tom Beal

"Smiles light up a person's eyes."

SEPTEMBER 23

SEPTEMBER 24

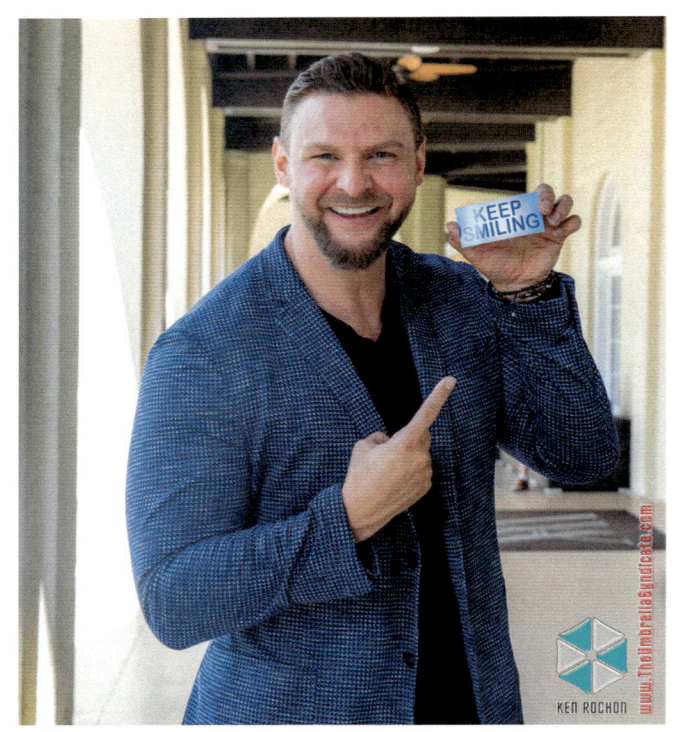

Kris Krohn

"Smile and the Universe Smiles Back."

SEPTEMBER 25

Laura Gutierrez Leon

"Smiles accelerate success."

SEPTEMBER 26

Jonathan Goldsmith, Actor

The Actor John Goldsmith has been in several television shows. However, his portrayal of the Most Interesting Man in the World for Dos Equis beer made him a social media icon as his images and commercials were viral.

"Don't waste a day without smiling."

SEPTEMBER 27

Cinnamon Alvarez, Author

"Smiling will charge up your day because it is electrifying!"

SEPTEMBER 28

SEPTEMBER 29

Jay Baer, Founder Convince & Convert

As a digital media marketing industry leader, international speaker and NY Times best-selling author focuses on excellence through his new book: *Hug Your Haters*.

"Sometimes all it takes is a smile to make everything feel better."

SEPTEMBER 30

OCTOBER 1

Gerald Smiley

"Everyone smiles in the same language."

OCTOBER 2

Hilton Felton IV

"Smiles are like bacon, everyone loves them."

OCTOBER 3

OCTOBER 4

Captain Lou Edwards

"A smile is the shortest distance between two people."

OCTOBER 5

Dr. Louis Bon-Ami

"I don't always smile, but when I do,
I love to hold this Keep Smiling Card."

OCTOBER 6

AJ Puedan

"Let your smile change the world,
but don't let the world change your smile."

OCTOBER 7

Nicole (Nikki) Ari Parker-Kodjoe, Actress & Model

Nikki Kodjoe is a model and actress most known for her role in *Boogie Nights* as Becky Barnett.

"The best way to start your day is with a smile. That is also the best way to end it. :)"

OCTOBER 8

Karl Bryan

"Only sunshine is brighter than your smile."

OCTOBER 9

John Fitzgerald Booty

"Smiling is my favorite exercise."

OCTOBER 10

Crystal Kingsbury Foss, Model

"Count your age by friends, not years. Count your life by smiles, not tears."

OCTOBER 11

Max Major

"A cat may have your tongue, but a smile can always prevail."

OCTOBER 12

OCTOBER 13

Tonino Lamborghini

"The secret to longevity is to smile as often as possible."

OCTOBER 14

OCTOBER 15

Kevin Harrington, Original Shark Tank Member

Kevin Harrington, one of the original Shark Tank members, is a serial entrepreneur most known for his "Seen on TV' infomercials.

"A smile is a strategic way of causing a positive moment and movement."

OCTOBER 16

OCTOBER 17

Michelle Mras

"A Smile is the best way to hypnotize the world to respond with happiness."

OCTOBER 18

Dr. Reneé Starlynn Allen

Quiet time with yourself is essential to reflect on your inner smile and your voice you did not hear because of your cluttered mind. Allow your mind to wander within yourself.

OCTOBER 19

Dr. Nadia Linda Hole, QiGong Master for Secrets of QiGong Masters

"10X Your Smiles and 10X Your Success!"

OCTOBER 20

Michael Sturba, CEO Micro Puzzle

"Use your smile to change the world.
Do not let the world change your smile."

OCTOBER 21

Morgan Workman, Gift of Movement

"An inner smile is essential, as the ancestors say, The teeth are smiling, but is the heart."

295

OCTOBER 22

OCTOBER 23

Teresa de Grosbois

"Smile and Ka-Ching you attract more love and opportunities."

OCTOBER 24

OCTOBER 25

OCTOBER 26

Ken Van Liew

"A smile is the light in your window that tells others that there is a caring, sharing person inside."
~ Denis Waitley

OCTOBER 27

Lee Greenwood

American country music artist. Active since 1962, he has released more than 20 major-label albums and has charted more than 35 singles on the Billboard country music charts.

"A smile is a curve that sets everything straight."

OCTOBER 28

OCTOBER 29

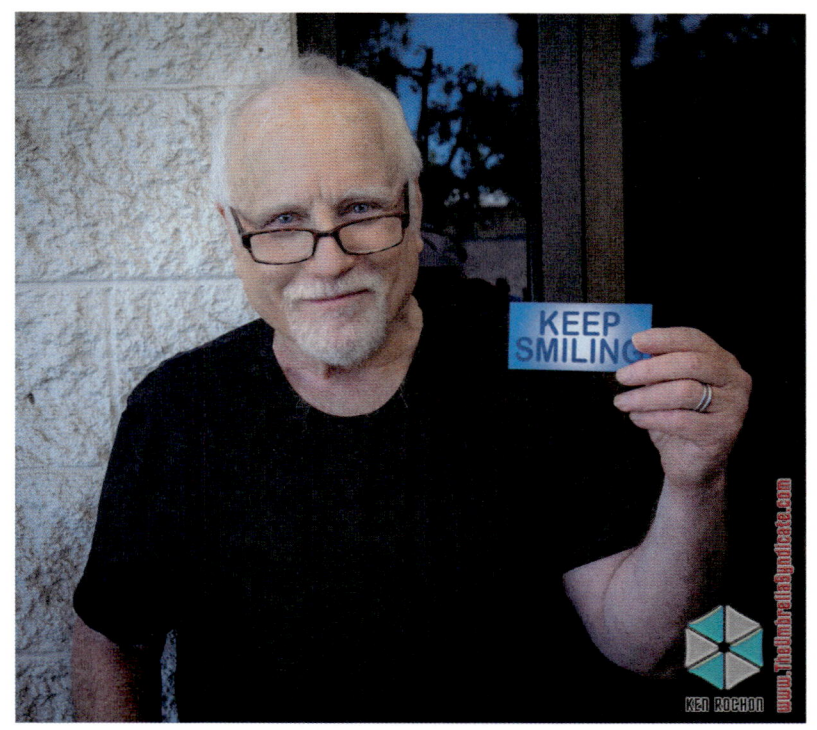

Richard Dreyfuss

"Illuminate your smile."

OCTOBER 30

OCTOBER 31

NOVEMBER 1

NOVEMBER 2

NOVEMBER 3

J. Scott Reib

"A simple smile. That's the start of opening your heart and being compassionate to others."
– Dalai Lama

NOVEMBER 4

Matthew McConaughey

American actor and producer. He first gained notice for his supporting performance in the coming-of-age comedy Dazed and Confused, which is considered by many to be the actor's breakout role.

"Let your smile change the world, but don't let the world change your smile."

NOVEMBER 5

NOVEMBER 6

Faye Kovler Kitariev

"The greatest self is a peaceful smile, that always sees the world smiling back." ~ Bryant H. McGill

NOVEMBER 7

Cintia Hullen

"A smile is the best makeup any girl can wear."

NOVEMBER 8

NOVEMBER 9

Mike Lewis

"Smiling resets your mood."

NOVEMBER 10

Aimmee Kodachian

"Because of your smile, you make life more beautiful." –Thich Nhat Hanh

NOVEMBER 11

Jeffrey Hayzlett

"Swing that frown pendulum to a Smile."

NOVEMBER 12

Katherine McIntosh

"Best Ships are Friendships with Smiles."

NOVEMBER 13

Royal Highness Crown Princess Katherine, Princess of Serbia

"Let us always meet each other with smile, for the smile is the beginning of love." – Mother Teresa

NOVEMBER 14

Matthew Gibbons

"Smile! And that's an order!"

NOVEMBER 15

John Duffy

"Whatever comes in my way,
I take it with a smile."

NOVEMBER 16

Bernardo Moya

"Life is like a mirror, we get the best results when we smile at it."

NOVEMBER 17

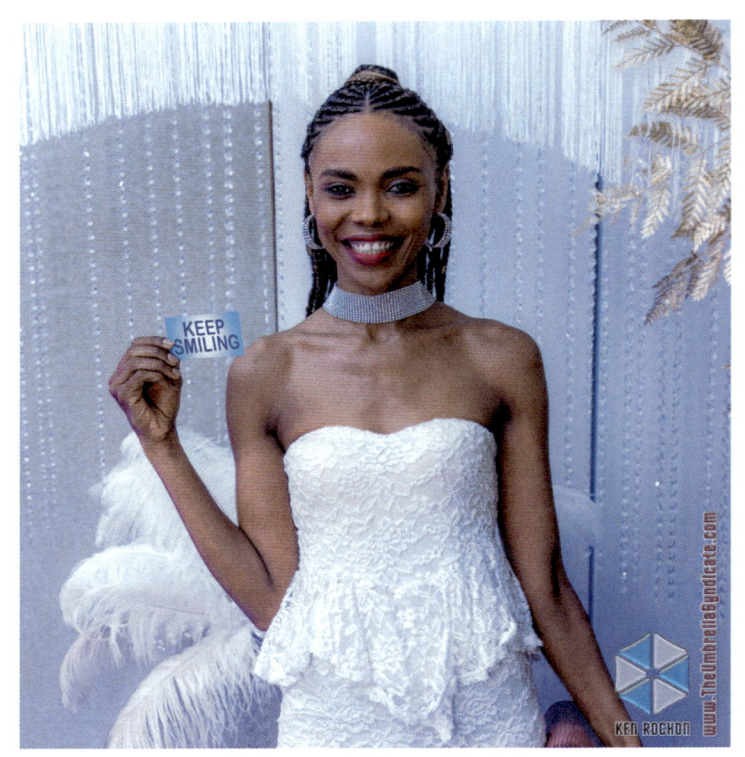

Selamawit Yirga, Model

"Smile Like an Egyptian."

NOVEMBER 18

NOVEMBER 19

Peter Anthony Wynn

"A smile is like beautiful poetry. It makes every aspect of your face dance with energy."
~ Ken Rochon

NOVEMBER 20

NOVEMBER 21

NOVEMBER 22

Ray Leonard, Jr., Speaker

"I have never seen a smiling face that was not beautiful."

NOVEMBER 23

NOVEMBER 24

Jen Du Plessis

"Keep smiling and be happy."

NOVEMBER 25

NOVEMBER 26

Dolf de Roos

"A smile is the universal welcome."
– Max Eastman

NOVEMBER 27

Larry Steinhouse

"Smile despite the circumstances and laugh throughout the pain. Life is full of hardships but it is how you deal with them that will define you."

NOVEMBER 28

Craig Duswalt, Author & Speaker

"Smile when you speak and you will speak with love."

Petri Byrd

"I love smiling. Smiling is my favorite."

NOVEMBER 30

Hugh Brockington

"Share your smile with the world. It's a symbol of friendship and peace." – Christie Brinkley

DECEMBER 1

Donny Boaz

"Master your smile and you will be servant to no one."

DECEMBER 2

Barry Shore

"A room full of smiles is the ultimate dream room!" – Ken Rochon, Jr.

DECEMBER 3

Randy Sutton

"Show the Smile of your Soul, and Heal the World." – Ken Rochon, Jr.

DECEMBER 4

Doug Sandler, Author

"Keep walking and keep smiling." – Tiny Tim

DECEMBER 5

Micah Fitzgerald, Actor

"Smile and you will Live Life Grand."

DECEMBER 6

Angelina Cortez

"It takes 26 muscles to smile, and 62 muscles to frown."

DECEMBER 7

Dave Chametzky

"A big smile is a happy heart."

DECEMBER 8

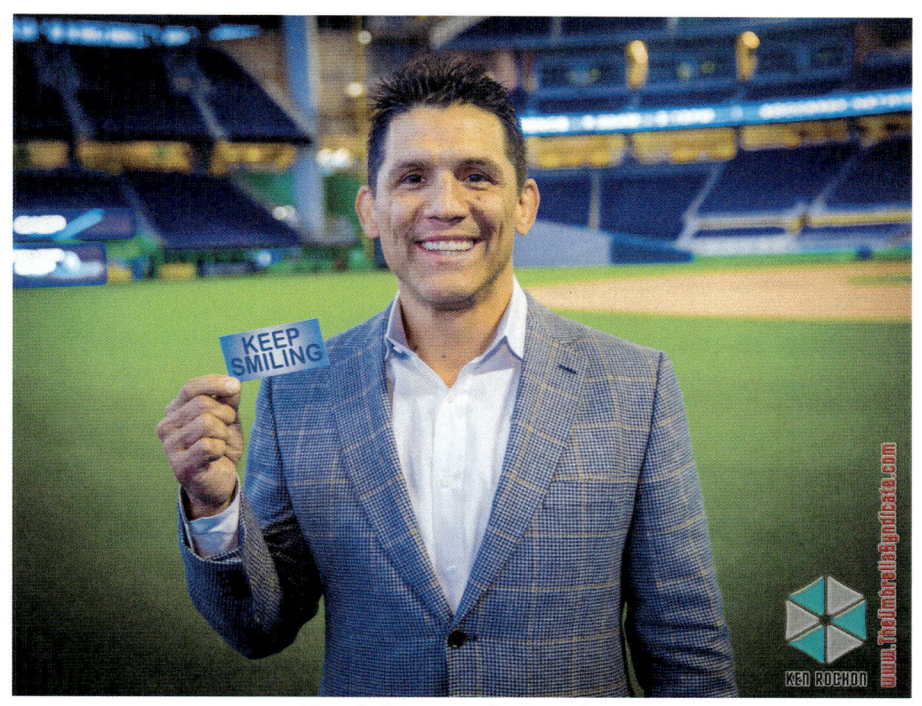

Frank Shamrock, Speaker

"Speakers smile and their message is heard better."

DECEMBER 9

DECEMBER 10

Satnam Singh Bhamara

"Swing that frown pendulum to a Smile."

DECEMBER 11

Jermaine Jackson

"Your attitude reflects the smile you wear every minute of the day."

DECEMBER 12

Allan Karl

"Smile. Let everyone know that today, you're a lot stronger than you were yesterday."

DECEMBER 13

David Fagan

"The best thing you can produce in the world is a smile that inspires others."

DECEMBER 14

Jim Britt

"Keep calm and keep smiling!"

DECEMBER 15

Steve Stealth Miller

"Smile! It increases your face value."
– Robert Harling

DECEMBER 16

DECEMBER 17

Arkevious Armstrong

"I want to touch the heart of the world and make it smile."

DECEMBER 18

Eric Jones, Author

"Wrinkles should merely indicate where smiles have been." – Mark Twain

DECEMBER 19

DECEMBER 20

Gerard Adams

"Smile and be kind, for we are here in this world just for a while."

DECEMBER 21

Andrea Partee

"Smile 'til your silly."

DECEMBER 22

LuAn Mitchell

"A woman is most beautiful when she smiles."

DECEMBER 23

DECEMBER 24

DECEMBER 25

Noel Lee, CEO, Monster, Inc. & Engineer

Noel Lee, former drummer, is CEO of Monster Inc. which is the largest company focused on cables and wires that assure the highest functionality in audio electronics.

"Smiling is Kentagious!"

DECEMBER 26

Cathy Droz, Author

"Let my soul smile through my heart and my heart smile through my eyes, that I may scatter rich smiles in sad hearts." – Paramahansa Yogananda

DECEMBER 27

DECEMBER 28

Dr. John Gray, Author

Relationship consultant, John Gray, penned the best-selling book, *"Women are from Venus, Men are from Mars."* He is a sought-after speaker.

"Smiles create harmony with Mars & Venus."

DECEMBER 29

Sahara Rahas

"Make smiling a habit!"

DECEMBER 30

Henry Cho

"I like sharing a smile… it always keeps getting shared."

DECEMBER 31

JR Spear, Author, Founder of BLN, Veteran

"Amplify Your Smile!"

INDEX

Aaron Velky	237
Adam Wilber	31
Aidan Uttinger	77
Aimmee Kodachian	315
Ajit Nawalkha	242
AJ Puedan	280
AJ Smith	72
Alexi Lalas, USMNT	153
Allan Karl	347
Amberly Brown Lago	76
Amberlyn White	230
Amy Wake	42
Andrea Adams Miller	125
Andrea Partee	356
Andre Berto	251
Andrew Zimmern	186
Angelina Cortez	341
Angel Ribo	223
Angel Tuccy	200
Anik Singal	166
Anna Pereira	57
Antoine Chevalier	56
Arkevious Armstrong	352
Artis Leon Ivey Jr., AKA Coolio	214
Ashkan Tabibnia	227
Austin J. Haines	51
Austin LeFevre	263
Barry Shore	337
Becca Tebon	78
Ben Ward	168
Bernardo Moya	321
Bill Walsh	258
Bob Burg	29
Brandon Steiner	175
Brent Stone	53
Bret Michaels	75
Brian Kelly	244
Brian Tracy	5
Bruce Davison	180
Butch Patrick	215
Buzz Aldrin	20
Captain Lou Edwards	278
Carl Gould	228
Carlos Siqueira	26
Carl Weathers	14
Cathy Droz	361
Cemo Basen	50
Chandler E. Bolt	138
Chuck Negron	160
Cinnamon Alvarez	271
Cintia Hullen	312
Clarissa Burt	116
Claudia Wells	187
Clifton Crosby	261
Coach Ken Carter	44
Corinne Hancock	194

Craig Duswalt	333
Crystal Kingsbury Foss	284
CSM Donnell Johns	117
Dame Lillian Walker	129
Dan Fleyshman	245
Dan Henry	185
Daniela Peeler	246
Daniel Pink	205
Dave Chametzky	342
Dave Farrow	10
David Bayer	213
David Fagan	348
David Tutera	114
David Wolfe	219
Daymond John	54
D. Bliss Verrengia	62
Demond Nicholson	46
Devin Scott	21
Diane Halfman	12
Dolf de Roos	331
Dom Faussette	34
Doni Glover	179
Donny Boaz	336
Doug Sandler	339
Dr. Bill Dorfman	260
Dr. Brett Lane aka 'Dr. Digital'	163
Dr. Cheryl Lentz	135
Dr. Clint Rogers	68
Dr. Craig Coates	191
Dr. Freeman Hrabowski III	226
Dr. Greg S. Reid	217
Dr. Ivan Misner	182
Dr. James Dentley	39
Dr. John Gray	363
Dr. Kara Scott Dentley	256
Dr. Lotus Riché	248
Dr. Louis Bon-Ami	279
Dr. Nadia Linda Hole	293
Dr. Nate Salah	206
Dr. Reneé Starlynn Allen	292
Dr. Rich Castellano	249
Dr. Robert Cialdini	118
Dr. Sarah Langley	28
Dr. Sher Mathew	123
Dr. Steve Taubman	156
Dr. Vinny Leonti	143
Dr. Will Moreland	22
Dupé Aleru	170
Elle MacPherson	89
Eric Jones	353
Erin Ley	69
Faye Kovler Kitariev	311
Frank Kern	243
Frank Shamrock	343
George C. Fraser	122
George Takei	111
Gerald Patrick Mathers	154
Gerald Smiley	275
Gerard Adams	355
Gift Hughes	204
Gina Gaudio-Graves	157
Gizelle Bryant	253

KEEP SMILING: BIRTHDAYS HAPPENS!

Gov. Larry Hogan	146
Grant Cardone	81
Gretchen Downey	61
Gualter Amarelo	58
Guy "Master Gee" O'Brien	167
Harper Grace	178
Harry Lay, CEO	130
Helice 'Grandma Sparky' Bridges	91
Henry Cho	365
Hershal Walker	63
Hilton Felton IV	276
Huey Scott	113
Hugh Brockington	335
Ilana Bissonnette	131
Isaiah Washington	216
Jack Canfield	232
Jackson Strong	149
James Lawrence	98
Jane Deuber	17
Jay Abraham	8
Jay Baer	273
Jay Fiset	27
Jay Ghanashyam Shetty	250
Jay Jay French	202
Jeff Parker	255
Jeffrey Hayzlett	316
Jehanne de Champvallon	174
Jen Du Plessis	329
Jenny Powers	41
Jermaine Jackson	346
Jerry DJSkeeper Cleo	93
Jesse Cruz	43
Jewels Muller	212
Jim Britt	349
Jim Koch	148
JJ Villar	70
Joel Comm	126
Joe Piscopo	169
John Assaraf	1
John Duffy	320
John Fitzgerald Booty	283
John Hope Bryant	37
John Paul DeJoria	104
John Travolta	49
Jonathan Goldsmith	270
Jon Block	183
José Andrés	195
Jose Escobar	25
Joy Cooper Willett	112
JR Spear	366
J. Scott Reib	308
Kameren Dawson	71
Karen Owens	73
Karl Bryan	282
Kate Abdo, Fox Sports	252
Katherine McIntosh	317
Ken Davitian	171
Ken 'Dr. Smiley' Rochon, Jr., PhD	218, 379
Ken McArthur	199
Kenny Aronoff	67
Kenny Harper	151
Ken Van Liew	300

Name	Page
Kevin Harrington	289
Kris Krohn	268
Kyle Arrington	225
Lance Allred	33
Landon Timothy Donovan, USMNT	64
Larry Steinhouse	332
Larry Wilcox	221
Laura Clark	162
Laura Gutierrez Leon	269
Lawrence Taylor	35
Leah Roling	208
Lee Greenwood	301
Leeza Gibbons	86
Leggra Colon	16
Leo Climaco	32
Les Brown	48
Linda Bruns	82
Lizzie Ens	231
Lowell Sheets	36
Lt. General Russel L. Honoré	259
LuAn Mitchell	357
Luis Guzmán	241
Lyman A. Montgomery	177
Maggy Fancy Francois	139
Maimah Karmo	127
Mali Phonpadith	84
Mandy White Eskelin	97
Manny Lopez	80
Maria Matarelli	106
Marieo Foster	257
Mark Anthony Bates	4
Mark Porteous	159
Mark Volman	110
Matthew Gibbons	319
Matthew McConaughey	309
Max Major	285
Melody Garcia	107
Micah Fitzgerald	340
Michael Bernard Beckwith	203
Michael Gerber	172
Michael Maloney	92
Michael Sturba	294
Michelle Mras	291
Mike Lewis	314
Misty Bright	79
MJ McFarland	207
Morgan Workman	295
Naomi Judd	11
Neil Patel, Marketer	115
Nicole (Nikki) Ari Parker-Kodjoe	281
Nita Patel	65
Noah St John	38
Noel Lee	360
Olivia Black	15
Otis OJ Anderson-	18
Ouiwey Collins	88
Pam Grier	147
Pat O'Brien	45
Paula Fellingham	47
Paula 'Pixie' Dezzutti	155

KEEP SMILING: BIRTHDAYS HAPPENS!

Peter Anthony Wynn	324
Peter Michael Blicharz	222
Petri Byrd	334
Quincy Jones	74
Randi Zuckerberg	59
Randy Sutton	338
Ray Leonard, Jr.	327
Ray Lewis	136
Rev. Dr. George E. Holmes	229
Rey Perez	188
Richard Dreyfuss	303
Robert Allen	141
Robert Angel	164
Robert Clancy	119
Robert Pine	192
Ron Blackburn	254
Ron LeGrand	247
Roxie Griego	238
Royal Highness Crown Princess Katherine	318
Roy Smoothe	3
Rudy Mawer	173
Rudy Ruettiger	235
Ryan Mauldin	94
Sahara Rahas	364
Sara Bee, Model	264
Sarah Victory	66
Satnam Singh Bhamara	345
Scott Parazynski	210
Sean R. Callagy	24
Selamawit Yirga	322
Shellie Hunt	9
Shep Hyken	176
Shirley Luu	83
Sid Peddinti	140
Stephanie Frank	265
Stephen Howard	197
Steve Farber	7
Steven Gaffney	30
Steve Smith Sr.	133
Steve Stealth Miller	350
Stormy Wellington	52
Summer Dey	145
Tai Lopez	102
Tennille Morris	19
Terayle Marquis Hill	40
Teresa de Grosbois	297
Terha Watterson	124
Teri Miller	240
Thorald Koren	144
Titus Showers	165
Toby Keith	190
Tom Beal	266
Tonino Lamborghini	287
Tony Horton	184
Tracy Repchuk	105
Tyler Cerny	85
Walter O'Brien	55
Werner Berger	198
William Gary Busey	181

KEEP SMILING: BIRTHDAYS HAPPENS!

Ken 'Dr. Smiley' Rochon, Jr., PhD

"A smile amplifies goodness."
– Ken Rochon

ABOUT KEN ROCHON

Ken Rochon, Jr. is an internationally recognized dynamic speaker, author, social media expert and connector. He is a renaissance spiritual leader, who loves the arts, sciences and people.

After losing his mom to Alzheimer's disease in 2008, he searched for the ultimate meaning and purpose for his life. He prayed for a sign that would allow him to dedicate his life to service and utilize his skill sets to amplify leaders making a positive impact in the world.

Ken's ability to capture and captivate the human spirit at live events, on the radio, through speaking, photography and writing are highly recognized as evidenced in the multiple hundreds of reviews and recommendations. His love for his mom cause him to take more actions, which resulted in the sign he prayed for. His evidence was the avalanche multiple hundreds of 5-Star reviews and recommendations. Ken is creating a dynamic positive impact and building a legacy for himself and other leaders. He is Internationally recognized as an influencer that uses his gifts and creates platforms and systems to amplify the messages of leaders that desire to change the world.

KEN 'DR. SMILEY' ROCHON, JR., PhD

"Ken Rochon is a master at creating social proof. He and The Umbrella Syndicate team are fantastic with guests and really know how to connect everyone in the room. He consistently produces fantastic work and we are always so happy to have him speak and photograph at our You Will Change the World summits and masterminds," Peter Anthony Wynn, Founder, 'You Will Change the World'

The Umbrella Syndicate (TUS) was created, by Ken, with six elements represented by each segment of the umbrella that strategically and synergistically move the vision of a leader beyond their minds eye. He studied strategies of leveraging like-minded and like-hearted audiences to create these epic social proof campaigns for the leaders he chose to serve. Ken has created a formula that captures and catapults the message that wakes the world up with a positive frequency that inspires people to learn more.

"Ken and The Umbrella Team are probably the most proactive, positive and professional media team I have ever seen. If you want viral videos and photography, creative coverage and incredible insights into your event, brand, or persona. They are the top of the food chain." Dave Crane, Personality, Dubai.

Ken is a lifetime entrepreneur, starting in his teen years, founding and delivering excellence with the award-winning company Absolute

KEEP SMILING: BIRTHDAYS HAPPENS!

Entertainment. He continues as a visionary and leader with companies and movements such as; The Perfect Networker, Live Loco Love Studio, and The Perfect Publishing. Ken has authored 17 books on diverse topics; children, linguistics, marketing, networking, and travel. He has published over 50 solo and compilation books. His current book 'Keep Smiling Shift Happens!' has caused a movement of celebrities and leaders to join in helping remind the world positivity, with just a simple smile, attracts positive power.

"At the end of the day public relations, marketing are about communicating a story. The "HOW" is identical: Get customers. Move product. Drive revenue. Our WHY is what positions us to change the world. I love to travel because I learn so much about myself and others. I recently accomplished becoming a Centurion Traveler by experiencing over 100 countries. My favorite place to travel is back home. My son Kenny is the light of my life and a moment by moment inspiration of my purpose in life." Ken Rochon, Jr.

https://youtu.be/7lDcwQB0Fj4

WELCOME TO MY 360 SITE
NOW LET'S GET SOCIALLY CONNECTED

LEARN MORE

WEBSITE

- PLAY VIDEO
- CONTACT
- LINKEDIN
- FACEBOOK
- YOUTUBE
- RADIO SHOW
- BOOKS
- SMILE SPECIAL

KENNECT WITH KEN
KeepSmiling360.com

ABOUT ANDREA ADAMS-MILLER

Andrea Adams-Miller, CEO, The RED Carpet Connection, & Executive Director, the Keep Smiling Movement, Inc, is the machine behind your business that moves dreams into action resulting in a reality never dreamt possible.

With a whirlwind of energy, a passion for success, and a deep desire for long-lasting professional relationships, she makes the right connections, devises the best solutions, and implements the smartest marketing tactics to increase your Authority, Credibility, and Income in more ways than one!

Trust in Andrea to spotlight your business and find you the sponsors you deserve, and enlist Ken and Andrea to cover your RED Carpet conferences and grace your radio, television, and magazines to share how your event and the power of smiles, the universal expression of love, impact the world's Happiness Index.

Call Andrea 419-722-6931, AndreaAdamsMiller@TheREDCarpetConnection.com

GET PUBLICIZED,
GET PROMOTED,
BE PROFITABLE!

TheREDCarpetConnection.com
Publishing, Publicity, & Talent Agency

IT'S YOUR TIME TO STEP INTO THE SPOTLIGHT

Download Your FREE Publicity Campaign Checklist at
www.TheREDCarpetConnection.com

Andrea Adams-Miller,
AndreaAdamsMiller@TheREDCarpetConnection.com
PO BOX 443, Findlay, OH 45839
419-722-6931

Want to buy Keep Smiling?

Go to Amazon
https://goo.gl/CBckvm

For large qualities contact Ken@BIGeventsUSA.com and to learn about being the next author of the Keep Smiling Series.

Do You Have a Book In You that the World Needs to Read?

Imagine expanding the purpose of World Leaders in Dentistry by ordering your customized Leaders copy today.

PICTURE YOUR BOOK HERE

PERFECT PUBLISHING

Black and White

- Customized Cover
- 4-6 page chapter about how Smiles have changed your life / How you have changed someone's life by giving them a smile
- 1-2 page bio about you and your profession with contact info

100 Quantity – $2500
Additional 100 is only $995
Additional 400 is only $1995

Order today!

(202) 701-0911 • info@theumbrellasyndicate.com

Color

- **Name on Front Cover**
- Customized Cover
- 4-6 page chapter about how Smiles have changed your life / How you have changed someone's life by giving them a smile
- 1-2 page bio about you and your profession with contact info
- **50 customized photos of your patients holding 'Keep Smiling' cards included in the book.**

100 Quantity – $5000
Additional 100 is only $1995
Additional 400 is only $3495

Order today!

(202) 701-0911 • info@theumbrellasyndicate.com

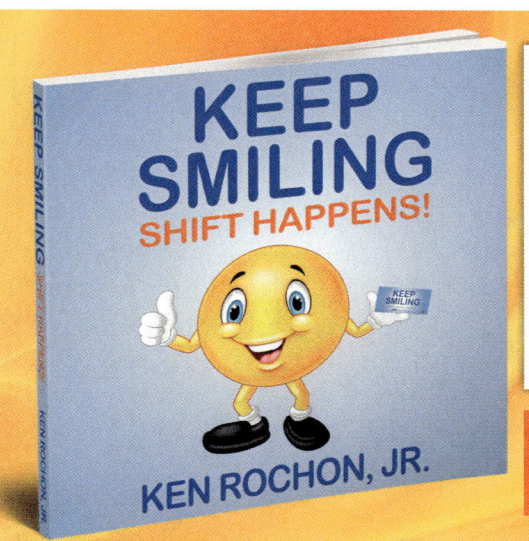

Want to be in our next edition?

- AUTHORS • SPEAKERS •
- LEADERS • ACTORS • ARTISTS •
- MODELS • MUSICIANS • DENTISTS •
- ORTHODONTIST •

LIVE • LOCO • LOVE
STUDIO

VISIT OUR STUDIO IN BALTIMORE OR DC AREA

ken@BIGeventsUSA.com | 202•701•0911

7513 Connelley Dr, Ste K, Hanover, MD 21076

THE ART OF SERIES
BY KEN ROCHON, JR.

More Books From **Perfect Publishing**

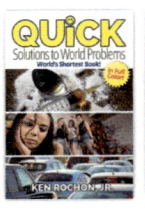

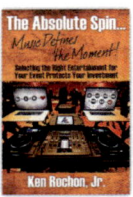

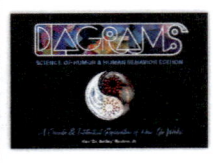

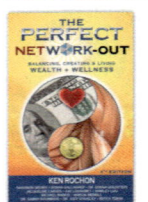

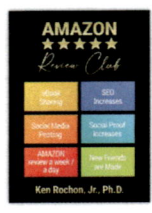

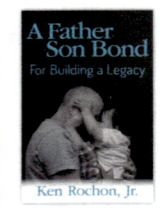

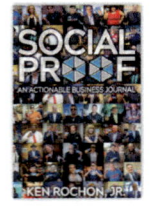

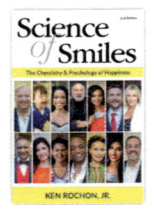

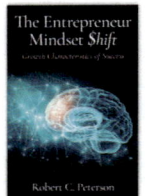

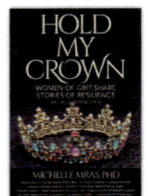

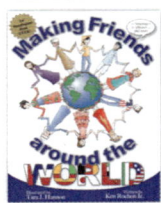

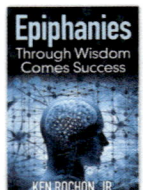

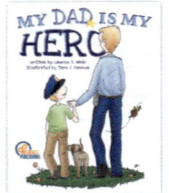

www.PerfectPublishing.com